myself invented
selected works

by keith jurow

Myself Invented
Selected Works

©2008 by Keith Jurow
All rights reserved.

No part of this book may be reproduced or transmitted in any form or by any means, graphic, electronic, or mechanical, including photocopying or recording, taping or any information storage retrieval system without the written permission of the author.

Published by Keith Jurow.

ISBN 978-0-578-03134-7

This book is a collection of poetry and creative writing that I have done over the years. It is a gathering of pieces written on everything from notepads to airplane sick bags; from the back of junk mail to the cardboard backing of spiral-bound notebooks.

Each piece is a snapshot of me. Each a piece of the whole.

I've written hundreds of pieces, but for this book I've chosen some of my favorites. I've been writing poetry since I was a kid, but it wasn't until around 1990 that I really started writing a lot outside of school assignments. I wrote constantly, especially after starting college. New environment. New brain food. Not to mention all the long bus rides to and from school. I had a pad and pen everywhere I went. Even on the night stand. My brain enjoyed waking me up constantly with an idea, an entire piece, or maybe just an itch. You never know when or where inspiration will strike.

Words can be anything you want. You can bend them, shape them, stretch their meaning, twist their emotion, and even fit the square block into the triangular hole with some poetic magic.

While looking back through all the writings to put this book together, the early stuff seemed very abstract and cerebral showing a hunger to respond to all the information that was around me. Some of those early pieces did find their way into this book, but many of them didn't make the cut. Not because they weren't strong pieces, but I just didn't feel they should be in this first book. Maybe next one.

Many pieces were written in one sitting. Some took longer. At first I would just write the date when starting something new. Years later I began writing the date and time. When you see an asterisk (*) in the date and/or time of a piece it shows when what follows it was written. This work is a timeline through my life. A kind of poetic journal. There are gaps because I either didn't include work from that time or there wasn't anything to add. I do keep a regular journal which seems to have gotten more attention recently than anything else.

The pages that say "blank page" are there to even out those pieces that take up more than one page; to maintain the spreads.

Originally the final piece of this book was "the contents of an unlikely story," but life doesn't stand still. And so, "squint," "cleaning heart," "what would it be like?," "check please," "feverish fields," "applesauce," "hollow," "i was happy," "aquamarine," and "no love" were added to this, my story.

Perhaps the only thing I'll ever have to show for this life, these days of mine, are the words in this book. In fact, I think this book may just save my life. Maybe it already has.

"Sometimes words can serve me well, and sometimes
words can go to hell for all that they do."

– HARRY CHAPIN

"Time showed me, you and I are not meant to be…
and it was only a dream that I had yesterday."

– JASON LINDNER

"I've come much too far for me now to find, the love that
I sought can never be mine."

– STEVIE WONDER

"I'm sitting at this table called love staring down at the irony of life. How come we've reached this fork in the road and yet it cuts like a knife?"

– FLIGHT OF THE CONCHORDS

"…and still somehow, it's love's illusions I recall.
I really don't know love at all."

– JONI MITCHELL

"She stayed with me just long enough to rescue me."

– JIMI HENDRIX

thank you...
amanda
kris
kristin
robin
ayana
laura
stephanie
suzanne
maureen
kristin

for filling my
mind
heart
life

table of contents

ember	9	please	48
void	10	pollen	49
golden	11	her reply	50
triple vision	12	gasp	51
final days ahead	14	it's dark	52
words per minute	16	like…	53
keep driving on	18	for now	54
esoteric flick	20	air	55
the flies	21	starless	56
nightscape	22	flight	57
seasons	24	just a dream	58
babble	25	scope	59
the concert	26	arms	60
what's the point of silent letters?	27	why bother?	61
are we what we are?	28	fever	62
dawn	29	a trap	63
different trains	30	drowning	64
fallen bird, scenes from the road	31	action	65
ten	32	beep	66
garbage bag under a yield sign	33	and still	67
my other sock	34	laura	68
now	35	ghost	69
before i forget	36	love, stop	70
mr. me and miss you	37	try	71
nice car	38	goodnight, anybody	72
moth	39	untitled	73
zap	40	echoes	74
flash	41	each and every	75
do you?	42	wither	76
what if?	43	wind and shore	77
kris	44	words can	78
we	45	metal and feathers	79
thinking of you	46	winter	80
sit	47	click	81

binary	82	broken	116
super paint girl	83	the spiders	117
untitled	84	ninja ballerina	118
bugs	85	robin	119
theory	86	sometimes	120
take a seat	87	goodbye	121
snapshot	88	nothing else	122
boom	89	turf	123
machine	90	a little horse	124
untame	91	short film	125
no more hope	92	untitled	126
precip	93	faster	127
words	94	stuck	128
flies	95	nostalgia	129
here	96	drawing a heart	130
from A to B	97	what is beautiful?	131
i'm no good	98	again	132
too late	99	misstep	133
train ride through the gray	100	water and earth	134
just words	101	miracles	135
somehow hope	102	first	136
if	103	submerged	137
joy	104	spiderweb	138
darn that dream	105	the contents of an unlikely story	140
taken	106	squint	144
tranquility	107	cleaning heart	145
run program	108	what would it be like?	146
searching	109	check please	148
same old me	110	feverish fields	149
if only	111	applesauce	150
just because	112	hollow	151
today	113	i was happy	152
necklace of desire	114	aquamarine	153
our final page	115	no love	154

ember

3/29/92
the end to an original poem entitled "Flare" 1992

TIME
RANDOMLY
EXPLODING
ENCHANTING
FOLDING
INTO
DUST

void

5/23/92

red air
gray clouds
wasteland

can barely walk
much less stand

i still move on
without fear

the wind still blows here

it's so clear to me now

city lights still burning
wind chimes whistle

flag poles stand
colors fading, dull

leaving the neon-blue hanger
out into a void

lost in ashes
and desolate convoys

buildings reach
to what once was the sky

towers float in forgotten seas
why?

NYC stands
beyond the pages of my mind

lying in my room
while flying

dust all around
starts to spin

shooting backwards
to the ending, beginning
the same
places change in time

golden
11/19/92

When time repeats, overlays
knowledge stands still while we move forward in space
Travel the cycle
to see a new beginning again...

With each new set of dew
she starts at what needs done
Though many, so often, has become few
is done, not easy, yet won

Losing track of existence
as the moments are all alike
Day to day, life to life
like a broken record, time

Relatives come and gone
The cycle takes its toll
Just as the Sun still sinks and rises dawn
all was only held within the earth
until the digging of the capsule

Aging hands encompass strength
In all journeys they've brought gold
Signs of wisdom continues
fades what has so long had strongly hold

The fire soon will serve to warm the soul
and there of within
A chair to take place that of movement
a blanket, that of skin

The morning, the dark, lies untouched
as only the wild perform their need
The walls are still, the roof sits cover
to the presence which once its shelter could feed

As nature sighs another breath
she dizzies with each passing turn of fate
For an instance, the air clears
as she awaits the next

triple vision
1/20/93

three shining suns
in three windows
on the building across the street

three people walking
two at hand
and one coming from the opposite direction
yet all of their feet are in sync

as they cross paths
as the light in the windows
becomes scattered
as the Sun goes down

planes fly overhead
their engines bring people alive
to the scent of their cause
aware of their flight
as if they might look back
to see if the glare
has been captured in glass
to aid the Moon
at the oncoming night

brick by brick remain
buildings they stand
constructed by hand
to keep out the rain

as the drummer upstairs
vibrates the chairs
as the Sun takes on a new shape
for the darers to stare at in threes...

a cop car passes as everyone dashes
to hide at the side of the road

blank page

final days ahead
1/3/94

car pulls up to an empty phone booth
the driver gets out
steps out of her car into the sunlight
the phone rings

she picks up the phone and wonders
how anyone could've known she was there?

on the other end she hears nothing
just the silence on the line
and the wind blowing through the cracks in the glass

she can hear the ocean in the receiver
it's a call from the water but the reception isn't clear
and the call is cut off as the Sun sets

her headlights seem to create the roadway as she drives on
the moonlight through the trees bends in the wind
she wonders how the Moon could've found her there?

on the radio she hears voices telling her of herself
and of the fire burning in her heart
to drive on forever

she doesn't notice the hitchhiker on the side of the road
standing against the wind
as boxes and paper fly around him

she isn't sure of where she's headed
only that the Sun hasn't found her yet
she races to beat it to the edge of the world
and drift off into space
away from herself

the hitchhiker remains frozen on the side of the road
with his hands at his sides
he wishes for a way to free himself
from the life he follows along the road
he waits for an open door
his wait is forever
the wind has taken his soul
and he now flies away with the boxes and paper
to play freely forever

the Sun rises
to find her alone
on the side of the road
out of gas
waiting for a ride that will never come
her face glows with hope
as the clouds cast shadows in her eyes

she waits forever
no one passes by
no one stops
she is tired

the Sun sets
she lays on the ground and looks up at the stars
she hears footsteps

she opens her eyes
as she walks over to herself
to see herself laying on the ground
she sees fire in her eyes

the wind finds her dreaming
and blows leaves and sand around her
as morning brings a new day she turns to dust
and drifts away in the breeze

the air becomes still for a moment
time continues counting
time continues counting
time continues counting
the Sun and Moon wait for one another
they wait forever as the Earth spins
and remains frozen in space
forever

words per minute
5/18/94

the words in a song go by so fast
just like the years in a life
at first you're a stranger in a new world
and then years have gone by
it's time to move on
and leave behind the kingdom you've built
the friends you've made
the world you know and that knows you

now everywhere else is a new world
in which you'll be the stranger again and again
the cycle continues
and the years go by
they go by so fast
that by the time you write them down
and transform them into words
they're strangers

blank page

keep driving on
5/19/94

driving home through the streets of a strange town
whether or not i've been here before doesn't matter
strange towns all look the same
my only guide is the dimly lit street signs
i do my best to follow their words
and i keep driving on

at the traffic light at the corner
i stop for the red glow
waiting to continue my journey home

then through the rain a man approaches my car
and he raises up his hand to show me something

in his hand is a copy of a magazine
one that i've never seen before
meanwhile he is trying to tell me something
that i cannot hear because the window is shut

with his eyes and his facial expressions
he urges me to open my mind
become aware of what he is conveying
and open the window to receive it in kind

without hesitating i raise up my hand
to show him that i have no interest
i don't know these streets
or the people that walk them
i'm only here for the moment
to wait for the light

he still wants to give me what he is holding
and tell me what he's got to say
by the look of the cover on the magazine
what he is trying to say appears to be real

still i shake my head
and wave my hand in rejection
then the light turns green
and i slowly pull away

as i do i can see his face
it shows that of a man who is disappointed
and that of a man who has been disappointed before
he has seen many closed windows and locked doors
and is tired of all the separation
and all the barriers

but my barriers are the result of uncertainty
and are in contrast to society's poison
with all the attacks
and all the set backs
it's hard to decide what to do anymore

so nailing it shut and locking it up
become our conversations
and the answers to everything

yet the answers are clouded
because the questions were never in focus

is being cautious helping to oppress?
is being scared causing people to jump to conclusions?
it's what you make of it, all a personal illusion

yet this man's face sticks in my head
i feel guilty for not reaching out my hand
to accept what it was
he was spending his time trying to do

he had a message
he had a voice
he had pictures and writings
he had beliefs
he had opinions
he had ideas
and he had visions
he piled all this together all ready for me
but what he didn't have was an open window
and all his words are gone
washed away in the rain as i keep driving on

esoteric flick
7/8/94

my love
in seas of green
it's plain and simple
yet not extreme

you travel far across barren plains
have i forgotten you?
my vision passes through you
through the red in your veins

hurry now
winter is coming soon my love

you shiver like a fragile leaf
stripped away and broken
taken by a thief
away from it all

be still, be forgotten
so that no one can find your weakness
so that nothing can steal your innocence

push them away with no more than my love
rather silent, something invisible
yet more than able to cope with momentary unbalance
between strong and weak
temporary and meek
seek the truth only within
your own world of meaning
no matter what happens
my love remains without words
only birds singing gives it away
so stay on my love
stay on the path
only the aftermath of the journey
reveals its purpose
in time
so continue on
stay within the lines
only through focusing on distant lights
can you find
my love

the flies
7/8/94

the flies in my head give a strange feeling
flying around frantically
looking for an exit
or perhaps even looking for a window
that they're so used to thinking does not exist
but are fooled by its invisibility
and take a chance and end up
seeing a flash that came out of nowhere
but it's too late to learn from their mistakes
or is it?

i guess the chance for freedom
outweighs the consequences
if any at all are even reflected upon
and so an act of blindness
not knowing how to escape the situation at hand
as we all jump the gun
we all feel around
for something that may or may not be there
on the other side of the blindfold
is there something in front of us?
or are we all doomed to
reach out in the darkness
when the Earth could be
a giant ball of glass
surrounding us invisibly?
waiting for us to jump or run nonstop
reaching out for what appears to be within our grasp
only too late do we find out
that a barrier lies between
here and there

but someday the glass may shatter
releasing all its contents out into a universe
with no end and no beginning
unless of course it's just a larger containment
or extension within itself
within itself
and beyond it is another of its kind
within itself
within itself

nightscape
7/22/94

while sitting here
thinking what to write about
i see a flash behind my closed blinds
as if a million cameras
were taking pictures through x-ray goggles
to see my face
why they've chosen me to study?
is just as puzzling
as their choice of places
but assumption can often be misguiding
as most humans are misguided
sounds of explosions
as heard on impact
aren't sighted when my room
is momentarily lighted
i feel the shake
and a wave of power
i'm surrounded by a stone-bound castle
but i'm out in the open, up in the tower
the lights flicker
even though the bulbs are in tight
what force of man or nature
could bring the brightness of day
into the darkness of night?
the Moon reflecting the Sun
isn't enough
even all the street lights combined
couldn't generate such a glow
and i'm kind of far from northern lights
giving the polar bears their daily show
what could it be?
a fluorescent sea?
perhaps the spark from the friction
between those in heavy static diction
i continue to be speechless
and breathless as well
everything freezes
as the phoenix breaks its shell
and flies through the sky
electrifying the dim

bringing streaks of energy
outside from within
these bolts of mystery
appear like a rip in the seams of the sky
and slice through the visible spectrum
until it radiates
and dissipates
until it's vaporized
and waiting for the next appearance
of such a random form
is pointless unless
you're the creator of storms

seasons

7/25/92

the world turns to dust when the Sun goes down
barren and void from town to town
a strong wind shifts the sands
and relocates in other lands

the world turns to stone when the Moon
is overcome by the Sun towards noon
the sky is lit beyond compare
only quick glances, no long stares

the world turns to clay when the planets are aligned
something never to be observed in our time
only make-believe makes it real
for those who accept fate and choose to kneel

the world turns to gold when the stars appear
electric spheres turn magnetic gears
the engine's noise penetrates our ears
while natives panic and throw spears

the world stops when its purpose is gone
and all are gone who rode upon
the universe will pack and board the bus
a window seat looking out into nothing
will keep it occupied avoiding fuss

babble

11/18/94

the is i you to stop go reverse must take every why do time late lost losing feeling break broken taking lust passionate ghost float base foundation court run blast hold real burst flow current rivers clouds almost timing rhyming steaming boiling hot guessing yes not much festive first only post when lights flicker tonight sure bye.

the concert

10/20/96

sitting still, breathing deep
taking advantage of a moment of low turbulence
a break in the chaos when the air is cool
when people breathing fire haven't found me yet
with their friends spitting smoke, making jokes
for the sole purpose of laughing out loud
while their rings of mist float away and disappear
i don't want to live in their world
where the air is heavy and eyes lack clarity
hands tremble without the warm comfort of headless spears
stabbing at their lungs, bleeding them slowly
surprising to find that the fabric of time and space ripples and cracks
when the magician makes his exit
cells crumble while inmates grab at their chests and gasp
surrounded by the harsh made fashionable
in the heart of the geyser we sweat from the steam
will the heat break and the fever subside?
will we ever be enlightened by plain colored skies and azure oceans?
are we calmed by the thick and the stench
of tired legs and a curbside bench?
in due time the Sun blazes the way until taken by the sky
as the birds wait still in the grass
like fallen leaves and fallen man
all adds up to form the sand

what's the point of silent letters?

11/11/96

what's the point of silent letters?
we don't hear too much from them
they're as quiet as distant whispers
and are as unknown as a small stitched hem

they don't jut out and weigh down words
or garble one's pronunciation
but they may leave someone with one raised brow
at why their tongue has no vibration?

are they shy or plain or timid?
explaining why they cling to others
maybe they are just bench warmers
waiting to sub for their sisters and brothers

perhaps they're there to make things fit
or to meet a quota or as an adhesive
it's hard to say, they hold real still
even when crowded they don't seem to give

like knives and such they sit and wait
just for fun to cut out space?
you have to admit we all want to be loved
and feel included and have a place

so silent letters don't talk at all
they don't seem bothered, they don't seem upset
but we're all waiting with cameras rolling
so far no sign of movement yet

are we what we are?

12/1/96

we're all just skin and bones and blood
in so much as nothing's new

we're all from the same pit of mud
our distance runs into the blue

we're all made of particles of dust
running scared from the inevitable broom

we're all just genes looking for lust
it's in the air, its job to loom

we're in tune with electrochemical reactions
infinite sparks in a complex net

we're all in a world broken into fractions
as the Sun rises we sink deeper in debt

we're cool, we're hot, both where and when
so why assume we've reached the end?

we're all just cells searching for food
to continue in our daily routine

we're all wanting to come unglued
with our fingers crossed we watch the screen

we're all the same in time and space
everyone and everything

we're all running at top speed to stay in place
at this rate we'll all feel the sting

we're too concerned and too naïve
always trying to change the course of time

we're stuck with nothing up our sleeve
except our journey's grit and grime

we're backward, forwards, strong and weak
all things end when no one speaks

dawn
2/12/97

in her mind the plane spins in flames
in her mind the car flips and ignites
in her mind the bomb explodes in anger
in her mind just flashing lights

in her days all filled with darkness
in her nights broken and down
in her heart a thin compassion
in her smile an upward frown

she knows there is strength somewhere, someplace
but the search has only uncovered pain
she knows that somehow she'll find someone
but the process is such a drain

in her mind the frost is forming
never to know a warming dawn
in her mind we await an ending
as the signal slows and is gone

different trains

1997
title taken from a Steve Reich composition

what runs through your mind when you close your eyes
do you envision pain
does it bring tension to your eyes, shut and flinching
what do you fear
is the world sneaking up on you
are you unable to look inside peacefully
are voices beyond earshot calling to you
do they ripple the air and vibrate your soul
can you clear your head and stare off into space
without wanting to look behind you before the journey is done
can sound spark your imagination
can you hear the coming train before it arrives
before it shakes the earth
can you stand on the tracks with closed eyes and trust your ears
will they hear the truth
will you be true to what they reveal
or will you open your eyes
will you run from the chaos in the air
or will you listen to its rhythm and let it vibrate your form
and let it ring in your head
and if you find a truth will you share it
will you share the air
or will you trap it inside and not let it continue on into the distance
to reach for the horizon which remains out of reach
will you let it drift off into space and add to the resonance of the infinite
or is it all just noise to you
do you rage inside, demanding silence
craving isolation from the screaming surroundings
pressing ever harder on your ears
weighing down on your shoulders
forcing you on your knees
demanding acknowledgement
demanding justification, demanding shape, demanding nothing at all...
it's what you make it
we each have different demons
we each have different drives
we all hear different trains

fallen bird
scenes from the road

5/2/98

fallen bird with its back to the sky
comes into focus as i approach
it doesn't shake or shutter as my tires blur past
with its beak pressed against the cold gray road

with each car racing by, its feathers flutter
an unanswered breeze continues to call
but the wings it once lifted and carried in easy conversation
are now still and silenced and drained of their once rich wisdom

those who take for granted the majesty of flight
cannot feel the pain when its story has ended
when feathers are lifeless and their keeper is grounded
fairytales lose their splendor as the sky sheds a tear

a stranded traveler without salvation
with no chance of hope in finding its way
now, long gone from my inquisitive gaze
i'm left with no answers
in the realm of the fallen, in this orange haze

ten
5/3/98

open spaces with strange new shadows
dance and flicker on soulful walls
in separate rooms with silent voices
as darkness haunts and breaks the calm
i lay in wonder of what she's thinking?
as her eyes grow heavy and fall towards sleep
or is she awake and trapped in thought
with no light to bring shape to what remains unseen?
the journey is long, to and from the horizon
and walks through the fields in the shadows of mountains
she chooses her path from a bag full of choices
one day to find that her heart always rang true
she has nothing to fear, the walls aren't thin
i'm only just changing her warmth into words
places i see in my head when she's near
yet i can hear her breathing as it flows around corners
i'm only guessing in enchanting seas
my travels haven't unmasked any final destination
is she one out of many, leaving me guessing?
or has all this already been written waiting to be read?

the cat seems oblivious to my watchful eyes
it plays as if the world spins without a sound
every so often a quick glance, then a pounce
and everything goes black as i smile inside

garbage bag under a yield sign

8/2/98

as i drive, the world goes by
and through the glass the distance stretches out of view
others try to take my place without knowing
that they're no closer than i in this metallic stew

i notice to the side a single garbage bag
underneath a yield sign, sitting still
it's a curious vision lasting only seconds
when my rearview is overtaken by a hill

the image however remains in my brain
a solitary object, an encasement of plastic
whatever exists inside remains unrevealed
or perhaps it just can't break through the twist-tied elastic

and why is this mass resting where it is?
an inverted triangle, standing in truth
perhaps put there by aliens, i am uncertain
and am certainly not a roadside sleuth

my other sock

11/14/98

am i here or am i there
am i main or am i spare
am i still or am i flair
am i constantly compared

am i in or am i out
am i spar or am i bout
am i sure or am i in doubt
am i forever to be without

am i sky or am i sea
am i seed or am i tree
am i lock or am i key
am i ever to be free

am i real or am i fake
am i give or am i take
am i go or am i brake
am i consistently awake

am i better or am i worse
am i wish or am i curse
am i silent or am i verse
am i to throw it in reverse

am i verse or am i silent
am i received or am i sent
am i kept or am i lent
am i finding ways to vent

am i brake or am i go
am i sun or am i snow
am i gloom or am i glow
am i me from head to toe

am i key or am i lock
am i one or am i flock
am i tick or am i tock
am i to find my other sock

am i doubt or am i sure
am i as i am or as i were
am i bark or am i purr
am i to see beyond the blur

am i flair or am i still
am i won't or am i will
am i coin or am i bill
am i ever to sit still...

so...

now

1/1999 2:40am

It's 2:40am and I'm just thinking about past accomplishments and new resolutions. None of it matters. No matter what we've done, we're always here now. No matter what we promise in days to come, we're always here now. The past isn't real. It no longer exists. The future isn't real. It has yet to exist. Now is the in-between. Now always exists. We must act now. We must find our way now. Now is the only truth. Time is continuous. Time has little relevance to "NOW," except that our time is limited. Each moment is quickly lived and then becomes a part of what once was. Now it's 2:51am. Now I'm tired...

before i forget

2/5/99

i have flown with you before
through the static filled stations
my fingers growing numb
trying to find a place
where you're unfamiliar

i have flown with you before
where antennas reach the clouds
my wings are fragile
and tire quickly, for i have no prey
just a need to soar

i have flown with you before
in an unending search for a moment of silence
the noise conquers the still
and you are hidden

i fly with you now, myself alone
across places we once were
my purpose is subsiding
time will soon catch me
and take my spare change

mr. me and miss you

3/7/99 11:05pm

i miss her when the sky is blue
and when the air is still and cool

i miss her when the clouds are thick
reflected in an ocean pool

i miss her when the lights are dim
and loneliness projects its curse

i miss her when my eyes grow heavy
and when the demons do their worst

i miss her when days seem routine
and nights in search of warmth alone

i miss her when my heart grows weary
in deciding to switch from pulse or tone

i miss her when the distance is felt
and when she is so far away

i miss her because love is pure
and colors brightly the neutral gray

nice car

4/8/99 1:37am

there's a man
in a suit
with a beamer
on the side
of the road
and he's pacing
back and forth
while the man
with the tow
does his thing

and that's all
that i see
as i pass
by the scene
in my old
beat up wreck
while the only
thought that comes
to my mind
is hey, nice car

moth
8/10/99 1:44am

There's a moth in my headlights as I wait for the traffic light to turn blue and yellow at the same time. There's nobody out here, and still I wait as if taking a chance would result in fuzz on the stations. Who knows? So I wait. The moth has no real need for this cold lightbulb sun that when prompted by switches will retreat into its metallic body until the next day becomes night and the road becomes dark, and street signs hide in the shadows; removing themselves from use as the Moon looks on. Its brightness is borrowed, however bright it may seem. It has no power, no juice of its own. So the moth continues its frantic flutter in the beams of my auto. Perhaps it is thirsty.

zap
8/11/99 12:33am

what in the world
makes connections in my brain
without a hum or a buzz
or the creak of old planks?

at no point in the process
is there a tickle or shiver
no pins and/or needles
sharp pain or blurred vision

for so little sensation
during the completion of circuits
only leads me to question
why the operator won't answer?

a sea of organic wires
entwined in relation to something
this electrical current
is making me itch

flash

8/23/99 12:46am

There are too many flashing lights in the darkness of my room. My eyes grow heavy and close, but the memory of the image of the flashing lights still remains with free reign of my head. The answering machine flashes with old messages not yet erased. The phone light flashes indicating a full charge. And every now and again the two flashing lights flash together as if deep in conversation, but I'm not included in their silent ons and offs as a man on the corner flashes some unsuspecting woman who then flashes her badge. So the flasher gets flashed by the bulb at the station for a shot of his mug, half full or half empty, at the diner on Main Street whose sign always flashes day and night without end, telling cars with flashing signals that they're open for business. No need to flash any money, they take plastic which is used to make flashlights, or perhaps a flash of light in the sky. An alien ship? in hot pursuit of Flash Gordon, who'll never stop for coffee at the diner on Main Street because his tape is rewinding as the display is flashing numbers in reverse as the truck backs up to drop off its cargo. It beeps as it goes. It beeps as it goes. But that's another story written backwards in mirrors.

do you?
4/28/00 1:18am

i don't have windows
i have walls
i don't have a ceiling
i have a floor above my head
the movement of others
shakes my days
the creaking with no peeking
water through pipes
like a river across the plain white sky
above my bed

i don't have answers
i have questions
i don't have an exit
i have hours that bleed into years
the ticking of clocks
reveals the one
the holding with no folding
my heart in flux
like a drenched cloth
being twisted and drained
of countless tears
yet a spark still nears

what if?

12/21/01 9:22pm

what if the fly that you eye on the wall
is the one that holds the secrets to everything?
the universe?
us all?

kris

4/12/02

what is it about you
that pulls at me
all the way from South Carolina?

when our only current ties
are words broken down into ones and zeros
and put back together to shine in our eyes

but so many years ago
perhaps unknowingly you touched my heart

i can't even begin to explain
how just for a moment i could see through your eyes
to stand in your sun and escape the rain

what is it about you
that pulls at me?
is it your thoughts, your heart?

maybe i'll never know
but i do hope that the Sun finds your skin
so you can feel how i do when within your glow

we

4/21/02

we are always who we are
does this take a lifetime to accept?
we scatter and we run for change
until we're pushed aside and deemed inept

after birth begins death
it starts to peel away at the rind
everyday we add up and grab for more
searching for room in our closets and mind

all while we wait for a comet or excuse
as to why we're all a mess?
and why there's no salvation into nothing?
and no check in the mail after we confess?

we join clubs and put a dollar in a cup
to save a soul, our soul, a spark
we continue to run with our heads cut off
and try to find our keys in the dark

we are who we are the day we're born
a block of marble, a block of ice
each day a go with mallet and chisel
hopefully we'll each carve something nice

thinking of you

5/5/02 around 2:00am

how is it that you're part of my everyday
when you're so many days away?

yet just thinking of you
makes me feel as if you're near

when the corners of your mouth
rise like the Sun
my world is brightened
and my skin warms

i can't imagine having you close
it seems impossible though i want it most

just a moment with you can fill a life
can fill a heart
i hope, i dream, i wonder, i yearn
to view the world from within your arms
though i know forever we'll be apart

sit
5/25/02

Aren't we all lost? All searching for something? Always changing, evolving, growing? If nothing else, life is a rollercoaster. And with each passing day our immortality wears away. Every day is a chance for greatness or failure. Whatever the outcome, we survive and hope that the struggles are met with happiness, a smile, an embrace, a feeling of love, or perhaps just a really comfortable chair.

please

5/26/02 12:57am

Her skin is silk; smooth and beautiful. It's difficult to find the words to describe touching her. It seems like something sacred. As if a woman's skin is something beyond sensuality, beyond feeling, beyond touch. As if you are touching life itself. It's electric, alive. It's warm, wonderful. Breathing quickens with excitement and slows in comfort.

How is any man even the slightest bit worthy of such wondrous things? Of such joy and contentment? To experience a woman's body is to lay in the Sun, to breathe life in your lungs, and fill your heart with forever.

I can almost feel her near me. She has been so far away for countless days, yet the experience of her still occupies my every day. How can I get to her? How can I reach her? I'm just worried that if I do find her, will she reach back?

The words I keep in my heart for her cannot be spoken through ink on paper, words on a screen, or a voice on the phone. They must be spoken when her breath is real and her voice fills the air around me. Then, when my heart finds its moment, those words will find her ears. There is still so much between now and then. So many hours. So many years. Please be there...

pollen

5/27/02

Pollen fell like snow today. In the breeze they flew, playfully, until they found a new place to settle; a new home; a new beginning. Some seemed as if they'd never touch ground. As if the light from the Sun was enough to feed them. And the air, no matter how slight, was enough to keep them afloat. They rise and fall outside my window. Some soaring fast. Others gradual and gentle. Some fly upward as if the sky had opened up and was pulling them away. So simple their lives. So simple yet beautiful. The birds sing as they follow the drifting pollen. Tiny white clouds of life. Soon they will blossom in fields both near and far. Oh what stories they'll tell. Maybe they'll tell one of a person who sat quietly watching as they'd play outside his window. How he'd watch with eyes wide and mouth curved towards the stars. Simple. Still. Perfect.

her reply

6/1/02 7:50pm

Above the treetops, no longer golden as the Sun goes down, big white clouds glow, set against the rich light blue of the sky. I blow a kiss in hope that one of these fluffy solar travelers will reach her sky and find her eyes, her lips. The world, my world, dims. Yet I'm still awake. I don't wish to be in the smoke filled rooms where the music drowns out the truth. Where the speakers shake and scream at the top of their electric lungs; spitting out distorted waves and crashing back-beats that sound more like a battering ram trying to get through a locked door behind a mesh grill than anything sonically pleasing. Where people are looking for something usually not found at the bottom of a glass. There must be a prize in one of them because the rounds keep coming. Maybe people do this to silence their days. It's too bad they're not out saving the world. Unless of course that is what fills their daily efforts. If so, the next round is on me. At least until the clouds come 'round again with a possible reply. Her reply.

gasp

6/1/02 11:35pm

No matter what happens in my days, whether good or bad, perhaps is needed to fill these pages. My choices, my fate, may be preordained, but my words are carvings; sculptures fashioned from the scraps of my existence. Perhaps each trapped within the rubble, leftovers from the blast, waiting to be freed; to escape reinvention; the continuing cycle of all that already is and may always be to form forever.

Or perhaps this is just an excuse to explain my actions. I'm smart. I'm stupid. Am I to be counted with the rest? I may only find answers in my last breath; or in her heart.

it's dark

6/2/02 11:00pm

it's dark, so dark
no spark, no spark
no outlet, no source
no signal, no signal
no direction, no course

i'm stuck, real stuck
no luck, no luck
no rung, no climb
no door, no door
no countdown, no time

all's lost, all lost
all frost, all frost
no push, no fight
no two, no one
it's dark, tonight

like...

6/6/02 12:42am

When I read poetry I get turned off when the writer uses a lot of comparisons in his or her work. When something is like something else: The wind was like... Her hair was like... The day was like... This can also be found in many a person's conversations: "It was like so bizarre." Why can't something just be bizarre?

Obviously you can't replace "Her hair was like golden wheat" with "Her hair was wheat." Such comparisons as "The rain was like ball bearings hitting my skin" could be stated differently: "The rain, heavy and piercing, bombarded my skin." Or something like that. Omitting the "like" can force you to be more directly descriptive instead of indirectly.

So why say what something is "LIKE" when you can say what it is? I do think that, when done correctly, a comparison can be effective. However, after extended use, especially in the same piece, it becomes annoying.

So remember, save the likes for things you like and be wary of the likes you like because they're like something else.

for now

6/6/02 1:15am

There's thunder and lightning and rain outside, but you're not here to hold me close. With each flash through my blinds I sit up and smile and hope they get my good side pose. With each crackle and crash, each rumble and boom, I wonder if you're still awake? My bed is big, but it's just me here alone within my room, breathing fast. The windows shake. The storm will pass. The wet will dry. The wind will blow away. But some other time, again it will find this place. Perhaps then in the day. What will life be when the rain returns and will I be the same? For now I'll lay back, shut my eyes, and listen for your name.

air

6/10/02 12:28am

the world grows silent
well, if not silent then muffled
underwater, almost weightless
my only hold on life i'm holding in
until i choose to come up and breathe
for now my eyes are closed
my skin, my body, doesn't feel wet, just held
as i hold still, not too much longer
soon nothing else will matter
as my brain cries out and my lungs demand my attention
they'll taunt me and disrupt my escape from the surface
i want to stay longer
but my imagination can only fill me with wonder
not with air
my thoughts can wander my head and signal my body
but the water holds me, close
it's gentle with its touch
my skin doesn't feel threatened, just soothed
hey, something just shook me
a big splash
it's probably those boys thinking they're funny
jumping in all together like one big cannonball
weighing a ton
okay, okay
game over
i'm done

starless

6/16/02 1:55am

my insides are being torn apart
it's like this everyday, or so it seems
that is, only when i'm awake or trying to sleep while my legs shake
have so many years caught up with me?
20's seem early, though they're starting to feel heavy on my bones
i'm lost
actually, i feel like i'm where i've always been, just watching the years go by
feeling my body respond as my mind questions and worries and ails
my skin is scarred and uneven in patches of red
i'm young and yet eroding, decaying
the mountains that reach for the sky seem like forever, while i turn to sand
if my body is so imperfect then what do the years ahead hold for me?
will i ever feel good?
it doesn't seem like i've had the chance just to be
nothing new i'm sure
i'm not the first to feel ragged, cold
i don't feel like i belong, anywhere
nowhere is home
i can't remember what home feels like
i do however remember her smile
i remember when i went to see if she was awake yet
in the spare bedroom at my father's house
she smiled at me
i can remember so many of her smiles
the way her eyes would close a little as her mouth curved
and her cheeks rose...
of all the things i'd like to do in this life, the thought of touching her skin
drowns out everything
what magic does touch hold?
does it set you free?
does it trap you in warmth?
does it steady your heart?
does it calm your breathing?
...ease your mind?
...let you sleep?
...make life, your life, something more?
does it feel like home?

i'd like to touch her skin before my eyelids become my only sky, starless.

flight
6/18/02 2:09am

sending her a letter
is like releasing a bird to the sky
freeing my words, giving them flight
and hoping that they find her sky, her eyes

a part of me is out in the world
away from my keeping, my protection

for her to read my thoughts
is to feel the wind through my feathers
the lift to my wings
to soar...

i hope for a sunny day

just a dream
6/20/02 12:35am

she is just a dream
what else can she be
when she is always on my mind
but never in sight?
my fingers are cold
her touch is foreign to my skin
when days and days away
no longer hold tight
but her world is not mine
our paths are separate and wide
she could be different or the same
or something in-between
my hope is fading
will i need to let her go?
i want so, but does she
when she is just a dream?

scōp•ē
6/22/02 12:36am

i've been invaded
by tubes and cameras and eyes
all breaking through my thin disguise
i cringed and twisted
both inside and out
my cries unnoticed, my strength in doubt
needles in place
yet they run dry
no drip or push, a cloudless sky
a day uneasy
though stretched in time
a crowd pushing through a shiny dime
my brain is thrashing
overwhelmed and bombarded
the world was much calmer before all this started
a quick flash and release
the signals are withdrawn
control reaffirmed in the fate of the pawn
life is still living
let's go for a drive
the extreme and the anguish lets you know you're alive

arms

6/23/02 1:29pm

my arms are open
just like it says on the neon sign
hanging in the window
its warm flicker is cold to the touch
but the door is unlocked and inviting

my arms are open
wide, panoramic
this space awaiting a loving invader
my feet are steady but are unsure
of the force of a possible embrace

my arms are open
no buttons or remote needed for access
no safety sensor in case they stick
or gauge to track the temperature
it's safe in here

my arms are open
still no reply or passer-by
soon they will shake
as the Earth's pull protests
the wind's attempt at love

my arms are open
yet now closer to my feet
soon my form will go from a "T" to an "i"
still recognizable, somewhat defeated
please hurry up and hold me

why bother?

6/23/02 11:24pm

why bother hoping
when doors are locked
why bother touching
when skin is pocked
why bother dreaming
when nights in sweat
why bother calming
when all's upset
why bother coping
when life's insane
why bother sunning
when drenched in rain
why bother reaching
when miles are long
why bother singing
when without a song
why bother excusing
when just because
why bother watching
when stuck on pause
why bother wasting
when time is short
why bother sailing
when tied to port

why bother loving
when another won't
why bother trying
when she says don't
why bother running
when there's no race
why bother smiling
when in disgrace
why bother going
when bones are brittle
why bother growing
when feeling little
why bother waiting
when days are thin
why bother defending
when made of tin
why bother calling
when lines are down
why bother joining
when out of town
why bother kissing
when lips are rough
why bother indeed
when i've had enough

fever

6/30/02 around 2:00am

fever burning, my eyes are boiling
the air is full, no space for me
i walk all dreary, my feet seem heavy
will i make it to my next cup of tea?
my heart is pounding, headache mounting
my temples overrun by the pressure of thieves
hope is flailing, no answers pending
cures wasted in the ashes of dying leaves
all just wishful thinking, you and i
voices muted as i dream aloud
legs are aching from constant pacing
affecting the motion of each passing cloud
as my neck stiffens from skyward gazes
i laugh at forever, still broken in two
health, an enigma, the heart trapped in the hedges
temperature soaring when the fever is you

a trap
6/30/02 10:36pm

The only thing that touches my skin is the wind. But sometimes the breezes get me twisted in a bind and bound me in circles, trap me in motion, and I tingle all over from the front to the hind. Without even asking it flies through my hair like a hawk through the canyons, a mountain or two, swerving and darting and braiding the air. It's hard not to blush, to stay mopish, stay blue. Maybe someday when the currents are still, skin will find skin. Two pulses a symphony. The waiting is chipping away, turning the present to gray as the universe converges on a singular me.

drowning

7/2/02 10:35pm

I'm drowning. For so many years I've been struggling for air. I kick my feet and move my legs and yet I still sink below the surface, swallowing water as my eyes burn. Nothing around me for what seems like miles, days, years. For now there only appears to be air and sea, above and below. It's cold. I shiver. No blanket. No embrace. Just the current. I can only see so far beneath me before the depths become haunting and dark. My insides are succumbing to the pressure. Sometimes I shake in response to the pain, the fear. No boats pass. Not in this story. Not in this world. The only sound is the wind howling around my wet ears. Voices are muffled each time I'm dipped under by the rhythm of the sea. Strange because the people I hear are nowhere around. I'm alone. My mind is overwhelmed and gets careless. It tries to hide the danger. It wonders why my feet don't talk to it anymore? It wonders why my fingers aren't tingling? It wonders why all it can see is black? It stops wondering.

action

7/12/02 2:45pm

I've always wondered what the future will be like? Not tomorrow or next week, but hundreds, thousands, hundreds of thousands of years from now. What dreams will be real? How will the world have changed? How will we have changed? What will exist that today we couldn't even imagine? What color will the sky be? Will there still be wars between people?.. nations?.. planets? Will the universe seem not so big?

What will music be like then? Will there still be friends?.. families?.. love? Will the beings of that time remember these days? Will we be their history? Or will we dim and go dark as our existence is added back to the Earth, the galaxy, the universe, the...

Everything that is, was, and will be already exists. It all just awaits a new configuration, with new possibilities and new stories to tell. Perhaps one day when all the stars go out, the last beings will know that there was happiness. Just to have a glimpse of life is extraordinary.

Today, our lives are but a blink to the cosmos. Millions of generations shall go by to the life of a star. We haven't even begun in their eyes. But still they shine. Warming us. Lighting us. Feeding us. And watching us. Let's give them a good show. They're not going anywhere for a while.

Action...

beep
7/28/02

you're the last, my heart's waiting for an ending
others may be well spoken in dreams
but nonetheless are spoken for in days
so many of my words erased
by the presence of another, taking my seat
i'm still new, but my world ages and is pushed forward
youth is evaporating, just count the rings
and let the machine pick up

and still

8/11/02 11:08pm

there are clouds in the sky
and the smooth surface of the water
is rippled by the current
and yet you only continue to grow more beautiful

your eyes have clarity and wisdom
your heart is heavy from many trying years
your hands are strong, as are your thoughts

and still your days, your story
has only just begun

live it well

laura

8/24/02 3:00am

her voice on the phone
is both gentle and alive
i felt a connection between us
apart from signals through wires
a harmony, a rhythm
her voice carried me through every conversation
she felt so close
yet reaching out for her would go unanswered
the space she fills is too far away
for my fingertips to find
is she everything in person as she is in words?
is she as warm as the sound of her breath in my ear?
i have seen her
moving in real time
smiling in the dim lighting of a club in the city
then lit by the neon in the cool night air
she is real
her name is Laura
Laura.

ghost
8/24/02 3:37pm

her body is warm
a blanket of skin
such beauty this one
oh, where to begin?

a living landscape
curving gently, soft
new worlds to explore
sensation aloft

i'm eager yet calm
she lulls with her eyes
what meanings exist
in this woman's skies?

all this a wonder
yet closer than most
my heart may just fill
oh, beautiful ghost

love, stop
8/24/02 around 11:00pm

love stop the teasing
this ride's beginning to jar
just when i think it's smooth sailing
you push me back to afar

i want, no i need
to feel warm in cold days
but you keep me just out of reach
after my pulse gets a raise

stop dangling hearts on a string
it just makes my legs ache
and when i think that i see her
you turn the shades to opaque

a glimpse is all you allow
a grain of sand consumed by the sea
as i sit and i dream
that one day she'll find me

so you see i'm still here
hoping that one day you'll slip
revealing your secrets and solutions
giving my radar a blip

try
8/25/02 11:51pm

she's sweet, she's funny, she's beautiful
her eyes are inquisitive and clear
her body, her skin, her vehicle is alluring
aching to be held or perhaps just in my wishes
what is she thinking when we're on the phone?
what is she thinking when i'm sitting close?
what is she dreaming when my thoughts are of her?
what is she feeling when i meet her gaze?
she's not everyday or a least that i've known
she's so many things and i'm so alone
i'll try to keep up so she knows that i'm here
but i think that she's more than any one could hold on

goodnight, anybody

8/29/02 2:10am

i've been crushed again
like an aluminum can
my contents, my heart having been consumed
my body, my shell, is empty, cold, used
i'm done

it's such a big world
and the missing pieces are scattered wide
i would settle to find just one, just her
a piece of the puzzle
but love is ever elusive

am i not alive?
am i not warm to the touch?
if i'm real then why does everything feel so jagged?
perhaps only her skin is smooth
yet my fingers feel nothing but the frozen air

i'm still breathing
and so there is still time
time to be crushed a million times more
time to wonder when it'll be the last time?
time to count the days until the end of time

goodnight, anybody

untitled

8/29/02 12:17pm

life is long, yet days are short
my thoughts keep bleeding with no sign of healing
she is vibrant and of the dreaming sort
but no wishing can stop my skin from peeling

faces blur, escaping form
only certain sparks stand out from the crowds
searching is threatened by each oncoming storm
but i'll look for a message in these words from the clouds

my so called heart can only flex so much
before it's torn away and loses heat
the winds are strong and alert with their freezing touch
the miles are rough on such tender feet

my body is my cell, my living cage
everyday on display as i walk repeating lines
the only escape is on the unwritten page
but i keep hitting zero when i get past the nines

echoes

8/31/02 11:51am

there are echoes in the world
in the air
in her voice
as words from my heart are returned to me

each and every

8/31/02 11:56pm

i love it when she wakes me up in the morning
when the first voice i hear is hers
when every word she says sounds beautiful because they're hers
her words are sweet, funny, and are for me
i love it when i hear my name from her lips
all else is muted
she's close

wither

9/8/02 11:33pm

the past is clouding my present
at every still moment the demons creep in
the fog thins from time to time
but when it is thick it seems as if it has always been so
i feel as if i'm running with elastic bands strapped to my back
the days are a struggle to get through
as the harder i run the stronger they resist
the past pulls on me
the years are flying by and yet my progress is faint
i'm aging and decaying while my triumphs are few
i can't find the answers or steady my hands
i never had the chance to bloom
when everything was scattered
and signals got crossed
letters unwritten
words unsaid
hearts unfeeling when the need was great
the rush and the push and the tears
the walls and the cold, the dark and the fading
the wind and the water and the shutter release
the blink and the passing, the silence, the strangeness
the once and the snapshot, the now and no more

wind and shore
9/11/02 12:51am

why can't i be beautiful in this world of mirrors
full of watching eyes?
will i ever know simple days
with gentle endings under calming skies?
is it even written in days ahead
moments yet unlived, the book of me?
who would know such things beyond the time of kings,
poetic tongues, and secrecy?
i'm only here, alive and real
from converging currents and a question mark
how else to explain i'm not, i am
an itch, a chill, from silence to spark?
but somewhere deep within the code
a glitch, a bug, a monkey wrench
has caused the weight of countless thoughts
to bombard the memory of a lakeside bench

words can

11/2/02 2:58pm

how is it that words can mean so much?
a dance of lines when ink and paper touch
when thoughts electric become static, real
emotions erupt to the surface to congeal

is there a formula, a method, a way?
a secret handshake beyond the eyes of day
to let us in on how the pieces fit?
perhaps a practice test or take-home kit?

all to find meaning within the heart
a reason, solution, a missing part
to how the letters get together
to form the truth within the leather?

hey, language flexes, bends, and twists
and the movement of eyes follows the movement of wrists
infinite options and colors, from red to blue
words can mean so much when they gather for you

metal and feathers

12/5/02 1:10am

The Sun through the trees falls across the road, forming shadows, zebra stripes in motion with the horses under my hood. A stampede of sorts until the light is lost and the stretch of road is again dead and cold as the vultures circle.

winter

12/5/02 8:53pm

Do you ever take the time to listen to your own breathing? Each breath in? Each breath out? The world slows down when you become aware of the life passing through your lungs; when you're in time with the rhythm in your veins. Yet how is it that you're able to affect the breath of another, even when you aren't near? How is it that just the thought of you quickens my breathing and at the same time fills me with comfort?

It's snowing here today. The air is frigid. At times the cold seems unending. But I know that your breath is warm. It keeps the ice from my skin; from my heart. Winter doesn't stand a chance.

click

2/4/03 8:05pm

hey there keeper of frozen time
guardian of the captured light of moments
seen only by one set of deep, bottomless eyes

skin smooth as silk, beyond words
while my heart skips a beat without you even trying

with a flash, a sudden beam, a jolt to the system
hits the silver at speeds too fast to notice

buttons pressed, levers and gears set in motion
to bring a memory into the visible spectrum

just wondering...

always looking forward

binary
2/15/03 10:10pm

the noise is unending, unrelenting
no walls can defend against this
i've failed in preventing
piles of paper, both seen and just felt
the fiery Sun pushes down, defenses just melt
the weight of the air doesn't object
to pushing me to the crust of this orb
clarity is stung by the wind and is taken
while the dirt becomes stuck for the skin to absorb
when does the quiet have a chance to be heard
with the crowds blocking the edges for the wise and their word?
contact is lessened between friends, between heroes
when our deepest thoughts are made up of some ones and some zeros

super paint girl

8/27/03
written by insernamere, used with permission

Super Paint Girl where are you?
mixing up your color goo?
bringing the plain and new to life
with your brush, your eye, your palette knife?

Super Paint Girl's got super paint
yet so many canvases are faint
i know you'll try to paint them all
changing the colors of winter to that of fall

Super Paint Girl use your super powers
so that we'll stop to smell the flowers
with your brushes in hand and canvas unfurled
oh please Amanda save the world

untitled
10/17/03 11:10pm

i'm full of dreams
both day and night
but my words don't always find a stage

as my time continues counting
from left to right
and my story fills another page

bugs
10/24/03 9:18am

bugs
they're everywhere
though seem mostly hidden when indoors
until that daring scramble across some brightly painted surface
reveals their position
and signals the swatter, then the splatter
adding to the color
not very aesthetic
though quite avoidable
if and when the concept of contrast
just happens to be the topic of an article
on the deadliest of our weapons
and the worst of their fears
a newspaper
an instrument of death in the hands of a human
if a bug were to read a headline or two
and live long enough to pass on the news
it'd learn that they're not the only ones near the top of our list
we're looking for terrorists
while we keep a firm grip on our high-tech,
rolled up, rapid-fire periodicals
waiting for movement
waiting…

theory

12/4/03 8:56am

Fate is based on convergence.
Every day we choose from an infinite set of possibilities
which continuously change the landscape of outcome.
The points at which the choices overlap or converge, that's fate.

take a seat

1/10/04 11:29pm

what does love look like?
do you need a description?
the color of her eyes
or perhaps her height?

she's beautiful in sunshine
when the hours are midway
and yet still fills the heart
when the hour is night

her hair flowing brown
and soft to the touch
plays wildly in breezes
a dance, a seduction

her smile leaves me gasping
it escapes plain recollection
even a nice glossy photo
is just a cold reproduction

her name sparks sensation
whether or not she is present
she's already left her mark
a sweet lingering scent

when will she hear
the three words i keep hidden?
i fear the opportunity
already came and went

so what does love look like?
well it's different for each
but some people can't see it
even when it's in bloom

i'm no expert, just guessing
my heart is still in its wrapper
and my name's still unspoken
here in love's waiting room

snapshot

2/8/04 11:02pm

i remember your face
but only in silver
still and unmoving
with an unbroken gaze

i remember your hair
as it sat on your shoulders
awaiting a dance
from those warm summer days

i remember your eyes
piercing and enchanting
always eagerly waiting
for them to meet mine

i remember your skin
from hello embracing
yet your interest was other
a space with a line

i remember you near
though the moments are aging
the years since the last
are growing and growing

my days are but dreams
as the hands keep on counting
but your heart left me here
without ever knowing

boom

3/9/04

When I was a child I didn't know what a bomhidit was.
Apparently my father always thought that my room looked like one.

machine

3/10/04 12:48am

when i close my eyes i can hear the machine
but i have to keep very still
at first i thought it was just a ringing in my ears
from all the years of horns and cheers
from strangers and familiar peers
but i think it's from the turning gears

is something, someone controlling my every move?
or perhaps creating the world i see?
maybe i'm not the one behind my own wheel
another being within the seal
mixing fluids together when i need to heal
tricking my senses to think, to feel
keeping in check what i deem real

did a madman let something slip between the cracks?
a noise or noises giving the truth away?
or am i just tired and needing sleep?
and overdue herding my counting sheep?
not wanting to hear that waking beep
though i'll still wander into the deep
without knowing if the drop off is steep?
or if my legs can make the leap?
i guess it's sometimes better my thoughts to keep
or seep out from a weary weep
though in the distance behind the heap
metal clanking continues to creep
shhh, did you hear that?

no, not a peep

untame

4/26/04 8:55pm
inspired by "Eternal Light" 2003 Oil on panel by Amanda Besl

the poet is lost
the lamp's glow is failing
or is she still smoking
using my light for a light?

she's thin yet she's strong
as her shirt smiles and smirks
with the face of a demon
in and around the silk on her skin

she looks to where i'm sitting
she seems on top of the moment
until she turns to walk to wherever
the shadows follow her for whatever
so much weight in her eyes
for someone as light as a feather

she's gone, but the door is left open
a slight breeze turns to come in
it bends and twists and finds my flame
and turns the room to black
she is gone again and again
and still untame

no more hope
5/9/04 2:30am (*5/9/04 10:40pm)

i'm going to fold up into nothing
when starless skies are all i see
i'll just lay down and close my eyes
and be consumed, no longer be

i'll feel this world remove itself
from every nerve, from every pore
my skin will dull as rhythms slow
as my brain cries out to save the core

no use in trying to delay the end
as my heart slows and slows and stops
no more saliva to wet my words
or sounds to hear in clicks and pops

and soon the corners will come together
as all the pieces start to bend
what was once elastic now turns brittle
any hope has gone without a friend

no more dreams to lead towards waking
no more sleep stuck around my mind
my world has stopped while yours is spinning
my story has expired, no click, no wind

*she said "i love you" only once
perhaps never again to find my ears
was it truth or just a moment?
some puzzles far outlast our years

precip

5/11/04 1:15am

the sky opened up last night
with the rain drops as words
engaging the ground in conversation
the sky had much to say
with the sudden brightness of day
in a flicker, a flash
the night air is awash
dark purple and gray
in the early hours of May
the ground reaches up with its bloom
and is answered in rhythm
electric and spray
but i cannot translate
for it's not native to my tongue
though dialogue and debate have been spoken among
those both inside and out puffing smoke in each lung
or perhaps it's a mist or a fog
or the distance to you
can't your arms hold me close
even with these violent heavens in view?
and this rock in my shoe?
so just before we embrace i'll get covered in glue
hopefully never to have an interruption in form
i await your reply in the heart of the storm

words

5/24/04 11:38pm (*7/16/04 10:24pm)

what are words but twisted lines?
sending shivers while flexing spines
written, typed, dictated, jotted
someday to find its surface rotted

sun and air and looming eyes
dancing 'round our inner skies
thoughtful, heavy, moving, still
sometimes crowded, avoiding chill

but will the endless hit the back cover?
and will she ever find a lover?
can't put it down, i've got to know
but words are gone when pages snow

she's still unwritten, the pages wait
her name is free from time and date
my words can't fill my empty shell
some thoughts only lips can tell

so words are real and so much more
they can brush the skin or reach the core
i hold them close, she and i, face to face
will i ever get to take their place?

she reads them and i'm still alive
now new versions can leave the hive
she may never see behind my thought
*her eyes, a net, my tongue is caught

flies

8/22/04 12:44am

i don't know how the flies found me?
i could swear that i killed the lights
what could possibly have given me away
when their status was absence for so many nights?

why do they circle for what seems an unend?
i can't get a position for each flight is random
do they plan their attacks in the smallest of war rooms?
is there a point in their path where their flutter is tandem?

a swing and a miss, my swatter is hopeless
their numbers are greater than my plastic weapon
they hit impossible angles yet with little precision
but can i truly be tactful with nothing to step on?

they buzz and they hum as they pass my defenses
i lose them in the clouds of my white painted ceiling
i know that their numbers will always outnumber
to survive without question and i've got a good feeling

here

9/2/04 9:11pm
inspired by "Custard" 2004 Oil on panel by Amanda Besl

help, my life is slipping from my hands
gray and lifeless, dripping to the cold floor
trying to return to the shadows, sunless
bleak, my skin is cold, i close the door
oh what a week, i'll have no more

i'm covered now, here in the black
shivering though my blood is warm
i'll wrap my arms around my knees
tight, no sting left in this swarm
unrelenting night, punishing this form

i surrender now, the canvas is full
containing as much sweat as paint
this gessoed flap once burly beige
now a masterpiece it surely ain't
cease i shall when my pulse grows faint

i'm only here until the shadows dry

from A to B

9/14/04 4:40pm (*2/13/05 1:13am, **2/13/05 8:48am)

when people are driving, other drivers are cars
*only circles of red behind a sea of stars
no skin only metal crowds each thin winding lane
how can lines of yellow even slightly contain?
no rules only instinct and the turn of a wheel
all it takes is a screech to consume all this steel
we don't care to notice any people inside
for when A becomes B then we finish the ride
life is not considered when we're turning the key
the road makes us careless and we all feel carefree
with anger and hatred when it's all just a trip
the road is an ocean with too many a ship
just one oops to end us in the blink of an eye
then we watch the others add fire to the sky
driving is a journey yet too soon to an end
maybe someday we'll walk **and be there for a friend

i'm no good

10/25/04 9:53pm

i'm no good with words
except when spoken in ink

i'm no good with love
i just can't complete the link

i'm no good with time
there never is enough

i'm no good with excess
i just get buried in stuff

i'm no good with anger
when it builds up inside

i'm no good with people
when all they do is chide

i'm no good with breathing
the rhythm escapes my lungs

i'm no good with advancing
i keep slipping off the rungs

i'm no good with anything
with hearts always out of reach

i'm no good with whatever
because it's different for each

too late
11/17/04 2:30am

your skin is warm, but winter's here
i think i may just need a coat
an icy path, a fallen tear
your voice is faint, a silent note

i mean to tell you once then twice
words that should mean more than most
thoughts are clear, tongues imprecise
too late to touch more than a ghost

i'm only here till time is gone
each second hand move pounds my ears
there's no one i can put my arms upon
the chance to find an answer nears?

train ride through the gray

3/18/05 10:00pm
inspired by a photograph taken by Ayana

was the snow here before we arrived?
how long will it stay after we've gone?
the tracks are covered, the trees are bare
somehow the wheels can still hold on

hard to imagine leaves in bloom
or anything more than this gray
drifts of white smudge the outside glass
yet the trees ever so gently sway

winter's hold seems here for good
for countless miles it's all that's there
yet comfort exists when skin is warm
awaiting me in eyes and flowing hair

she's somewhere sitting at the end
curled up in front of a crackling flame
the day is cold, but i'm inching closer
when her face will replace the sound of her name

just words

4/11/05 12:54am

It's interesting what we go through each day. So many faces. So often a struggle. There is good out there, yet it seems that most are content with the noise, the routine, the cold shallow hours that seem to fill time to overflow. What's it like just to be? Some desert island somewhere, where the Sun shines and the breeze cools, continues to be nothing more than a picture postcard, a fairytale, an untruth. If you've felt hurried, buried, wondering if the heart is real in what fills the eyes everyday then you know me. I seem to be nothing more than an observer. One of the few who sees. One of the many who can't fight the current, from here to the end. Life is quite a production. I'm waiting for the scene to end, the picture to fade, just to catch my breath. Still waiting.

So little breaks through the defenses when so much time has lent itself towards the building of the foundation. Walls so far and wide; a vast expanse of being scared, frightened, hurt, angry, lonely, tired, and hopeful. For some reason always hopeful because joy seems to peek in every now and again. A tease. A rush of electricity that sparks the core of me. Usually resulting in brighter skies. Unfortunately it's all but a glimpse, a whisper. Sometimes lingering. Sometimes faint. Never lasting. Never truly real. Just a hint of what may exist. Not in movies. Not in books. In life.

somehow hope

4/28/05 12:39am

we're only here until we're gone
brushing up against the shore
a grain of sand, a sparkling sea
things i try not to ignore

what if once was all we had
and time speeds up and passes by?
will the ends curve back around
and find us both under the sky?

my words are here until they fade
and i'm erased from ever being
but it's okay, the world is yours
words go beyond what eyes are seeing

soon ink to paper i will become
from heart to skin will find a way
pages filled and stories bleed
these lips grow silent, i cannot stay

the thunder outside brings the rain
hands are cold, the ride is long
somehow hope remains in sight
i know somewhere it will belong

if

5/10/05 2:13pm

if i could read a woman's face
and decipher all the subtle signs
a quick raise of eyebrows, something unspoken?
or maybe my decoder's broken

if i could feel her warm embrace
and give up what's between the lines
three words are all i'd need to hear
her sweet breath lingers in my ear

if i could only solve the case
and discover how she glows and shines?
i'd quickly reach for the nearest phone
and ask her why i'm so alone?

if i could find a way to end the chase
and navigate without disturbing mines
i may just find that open door
in search of her and nothing more

joy
5/10/05 9:21pm

if you've ever felt stronger, happier, warmer, calmer, safe...
then you know how i feel within your arms
it's a feeling that stays on the skin for days
it lingers, gently
until it slowly dissipates
leaving its temporary recipient dreaming of the next encounter
eagerly awaiting the next embrace
smiling at the possibility

darn that dream

5/15/05 1:02am
written while listening to Dexter Gordon's version

darn that dream
of me kissing you softly
our fingers intertwined
your skin is all i need for the day to unwind

darn that dream
of you finding me with your eyes
i touch your face oh so fine
and there it is, that certain chill that meets the spine

darn that dream
of you and i and all four arms
knowing both the to and from
feel free to squeeze till my feet are numb

darn that dream
of ways to tease me in days
i wish the Moon would soon beam its glow
darn that dream, how i love it so

taken

5/17/05 11:51am

when the Earth is taken by the Sun
in a circle we don't know where to run
the heat, the air, now weighs a ton
when the Earth is taken by the Sun

when the land is taken by the sky
and the clouds have all but hurried by
no longer grazing way up high
when the land is taken by the sky

when the roof is taken by the stars
an airless show from topless cars
frigid skin from here to Mars
when the roof is taken by the stars

when the world is taken by the void
and no one's left to feel annoyed
or underpaid or overjoyed
when the world is taken by the void

when this moment's taken by her hand
her eyes will slow the counting sand
nothing else can be so grand
my seal is broken, my heart's uncanned
the best of things always seem unplanned
with background music from some unknown band
her skin is soft and nicely tanned
her heart, a beacon, a good place to land

tranquility

5/18/05 1:00am

the Moon kept peeking at me through the clouds
on my long drive home tonight
i kept seeing its reflection on the hood of my car
metallic paint with beams of light

the Moon kept up, through twists and turns
it never seemed to flinch
i kept moving and darting and changing my lane
but it followed my path to the inch

the Moon kept shining as i kept driving
it kept the darkness at bay
i kept wondering how it lit up the sky
when i'm still several hours from day?

the Moon kept following as the miles clicked by
until my exit and my door
i kept looking up with my back on my bed
but the Moon found me no more

for there's no moon above where i sleep
a plain ceiling of moonless skies
but dreams they tease of days ahead
to again find your arms and meet your eyes

run program

5/22/05 6:40pm

the sweat stings my eyes
but the run was good
i've stopped and dropped my hood to breathe

i'm trying to slow my lungs
the air burns through
my heart is on fire too, it may soon burst

soon i'll retake control
of my pulse in every vein
reconnecting to my brain, again to feel

my hands have steadied
finally stopped shaking
my mind's stopped baking, oh what a rush

now i'm just sitting
thinking about the coming week
hoping for a peek at a friendly face

each and every run
really helps to clear the head
each day ending in a quiet bed of you to dream

two cats watch me sleep
i hear a steady calming purr
my hand gentle across their fur and i'm gone

searching

5/26/05 12:50am

if once is all that i get to be
just one moment between the land and the sea
a single glance, yet so sweet, the you to the me
and life pushes the days on ahead to the T

the Sun and the rain and the Moon and the stars
all reflect in your eyes as fireflies inside jars
it's so cruel yet beautiful that there's only one you
with your warmth in my heart all my skies are bright blue

i may never know how love finds a way?
the searching seems endless on too many a day
spin the wheel and who knows who'll win a connection?
but love's seats are elusive and i'm in the wrong section

so i'll sit and i'll watch this whole game unfold
and continue to write till my heart is too old
and by then my story will yellow and fade
yet from the feel of your arms i was never afraid

same old me

6/4/05 11:18am

perhaps these words need not be said
and i should just go on with my day
but a pad and pen wait by my bed
and they pull at what i have yet to say

the sky opened up and touched the ground
the time was night, i was alone
it started faintly then grew in sound
but such a thing is not unknown

i took it slow, the way was slick
so many times i've gone this road
bulbs and wires replace the candle's wick
and the now that of the days of old

yet my mind was on a different street
drifting gently, finding her arms
so much time between the time we meet
immune to potions, spells, and charms

is there a fate or just a spark?
this thirst, her eyes could so easily quench
still she isn't close here in the dark
just a warm embrace at some distant bench

to leave the Earth and search every star
arriving at some rusty martian pool
reflecting back my tears of reddish tar
would prove nothing more than i'm a fool

so i end where i began again and again
a new story about the same old me
if there's a happy ending please tell me when?
so that for once my heart can truly be

if only
6/5/05 10:52pm

your eyes are closed and i watch and grin
following the shape of your face with my eyes
soft and beautiful as again i begin
i'm staring, you're sleeping, the Sun's on the rise

i find myself smiling, you're captured, i'm trying
wanting to kiss your lips, but i can't seem to move
this passion is building as the nighttime is dying
can love be a question, is there something to prove?

to put my hand on your cheek, slowly to your chin
would cause a ripple, a wave, an electric attraction
or should i start at your feet and make my way past the shin?
you're just so many things and i feel like a fraction

i'd count every freckle and trace every curve
from your toes to your fingers and the landscape between
i'd explore every pore, every bit, every nerve
i'd gladly get stuck in this moment, blushing red, signal's green

i'd slow my progression only when nose to nose
so i can get lost only to get our hands intertwined
but these words aren't you, just a dream i suppose
the real you is elsewhere, but still on my mind

and suddenly night makes its way to the stage
no blanket this time, the summer's in bloom
maybe my thoughts will ease up as the hours do age
so far my heart's ticking, little hope for a boom

just because
6/18/05 11:28pm

why are sunsets so beautiful?
they're so far away
hanging above the horizon
the sky is on fire
something unreachable
a warmth no picture postcard can bring
a feeling no painting can stir
the day teases us until it's consumed by night
don't be afraid
it will return
to light your eyes
although you don't need any help to glow
you weaken the knees and melt the snow
though brief i think i may just know
the fireflies who steal the show
my pulse is quickened and spirits grow
counting the freckles oh so slow
while hands are soft and lights are low
it's nice to sit and find a pause
to know you're out there, and just because

today

6/23/05 7:42pm

sitting here at work, wondering why i feel so good?
what could it possibly be?
is it the weather or lack of a sweater?
just carpenter shorts, ankle socks, and a T

could've sworn i was feeling a bit under it all
wanting a pause, to step out of this day
and then a warm embrace and warming face
made my blue not want to stay

this feeling of you, having you near
holds the heart as i let my legs go
how such things are real and find me here?
a lifetime may pass before i know

being held and by chance doing the same
where both involved leave with a spark
to brighten eyes when the night arrives
and find the words to feed the dark

i'm only guessing at what's unwritten
each minute that passes just misses my stop
when your arms come together with me in the middle
the world may expand and expand and then pop

necklace of desire

9/27/05 12:30am
inspired by "Confection" 2002 Oil on panel by Amanda Besl

oh my, how sweet
i just can't get my fill
endless colors, doughnut-shaped
but just the size of a pill

i sweat as i hunger
and their coating rubs off
a tattoo of sugar
its former self brings a cough

my mouth is covered in red
my lips are surrounded
no not a make-up malfunction
my circus days have been grounded

this necklace of desire
is now missing a link
passers-by give a glance
but it's not what they think

my teeth aren't pointy
during the day i'm awake
i must feed this compulsion
my next victim is cake

i can't help this obsession
but why fight what's so right?
all day this choker's been teasin'
and still young is the night

our final page
10/8/05 6:28pm (*8/26/07 10:25pm)

i realize now why i met you
as much as i wanted to be in your arms, it was all just to soften my defenses
i think that we were meant to meet
and you were meant to break my heart
you were meant to leave me with nothing more than an ending
a final piece
knowing that questions will never be answered
and love will remain hidden
i can still remember being close to you
the suddenness of your leaving is a hard edge in my memory
a rock in the stream
so many thoughts forced to go around it
i don't think time will heal this one

first you filled my heart
and now all that is filled is the final page *of us

broken

1/5/06 3:00am

I'm having a breakdown. I'm cold. My whole body is shaking. I looked at myself in the mirror and my eyes were red and distant. I feel lost and completely alone. My hands won't keep still. I realize how isolated I've become. I don't know if I'll be able to sleep. I'm so scared. Everything here is so dark and still. Nothing is occupying my mind except for these overwhelming feelings of horror. I've buried myself in meaningless stuff instead of following my heart. And now so many feelings I've kept inside are erupting here in the dark. I'm tired of just being words. I'm tired of being on the outside of life. I'm tired of being so alone. But I only want to be with her. My heart is racing. I hope I make it through the night with my mind intact. Some sleep would be nice, but the demons are really doing their worst right now....help!

3:29am

HELP!
I can't get my brain to relax! I don't know what to do!
Breathe. Please just breathe.
I'll try.
If I'm still here in the morning I'll write more...

3:38am

Isolation.
I feel trapped with no one to help me through this!
It's night. It's quiet. Help!

4:04am

I remember so many things about you. So many moments with you.
When we met. So many smiles. Conversations.
It's been so difficult. You're so far away.
There's only one you. Sweet, beautiful, vibrant you.
My heart is with you.
I love you.

9:20am

I'm still here, though still feeling scared. I can't control my breathing or my heart. I paced the floor in the bedroom until 4 or 5:00am. I was so tired by then that I just fell asleep. I don't know if this madness will pass. You've held me all these years from so far away. But now that my feelings for you have broken their shell and are spilling out uncontrollably, you're nowhere near.

the spiders

1/24/06 9:10pm
inspired by "Untitled" (close-up of a girl's eye) 2002 Oil on panel by Amanda Besl

the spiders are trying to squeeze their way out
in slow motion they move as if just by a breeze
their arms are so many yet delicate and frail
to someone in a glimpse it might seem like a tease

see, my eyes are so bright that they follow the light
all together at once, but tandem they won't fit
all these guys think i'm flirty with my seductive lashes
but these appendages are far from any innocent knit

they reach and they struggle to free more than a whisper
but i don't want to lose such elegant features
i'll resist the tickling for as long as i'm able
but it's constant, they're restless for such tiny creatures

so i wait and i know their impatience will grow
and one day their army will all cross my view
then what will i say when my deep browns seem so plain?
after all, who'll believe a story so askew?

ninja ballerina

2/4/06 3:24pm
inspired by "Satyr" 2005 Oil on panel by Amanda Besl

i'm a ninja ballerina
ready to spring, ready to strike
graceful to the unknowing eye
each foot pointed like a spike

muscles tensed yet i feel relaxed
here in this corner i'm not afraid
only my shadow can get this close
it holds me with its caressing shade

i lunge forward, taking flight
barely creaking this wooden floor
a twirl, a turn, a twist, a sputter
arrows unsteady, yet eyes can't ignore

to find me again where walls meet
bodies lay flat across what was my path
my daily mission finds me shining in sweat
tomorrow can wait as i battle the sea, red with debris
it's my hair's turn to dance, from its ties it is free as i sink into a bath

robin
2/12/06 12:37am

sweet and warm
the heart is taken
by a loving swarm
no longer shaken
by a thunderstorm
my heart was failing
when without her arms
i need the railing

her eyes, her charms
are felt whenever she passes by
a beautiful woman, a dreaming guy
love doesn't need a reason why
her name, it soars and finds the sky
the clouds will part, my tears will dry

sometimes

2/12/06 9:50am

Sometimes you just have to let the heart say what it has to and hope that the world adjusts to it.

goodbye

3/7/06 12:20pm
inspired by "Goodbye" 2006 Oil on panel by Amanda Besl

why must i walk this balance beam
on my way away from him and his?
a moment that found me in my red high heels
this cold night leaves this girl a ms.

if the world is flat i'll find the edge
maybe that's where this line will go
how far until it's all made clear?
or they find blue stockings beneath the snow?

what's ahead is dark and draws me in
my heart is burning, my breath turns to frost
i really don't know where i'm going
but i guess i'm used to feeling lost

he said three words that echo still
but they were hollow and my tears ran dry
now he's miles behind and there he'll stay
he said he's sorry and i said goodbye

nothing else

3/11/06 10:47pm
inspired by "Olivia" 2006 Oil on panel by Amanda Besl

hold me water
hold me tight
hold me water
bend the light

hold my thoughts
hold them still
hold my mind
within the spill

hold each strand
hold every pore
hold my hand
and meet the shore

hold me gently
hold me in red
hold my gaze, overhead
a yellow blaze
and i'm okay
nothing else to say
your words are muffled
this dress is soaked
i'm full of you and all your jokes

i'm dead

turf

4/6/06 12:30am
inspired by "Playing Dead" 2006 Oil on panel by Amanda Besl

"i didn't do it!
this is how i found her
though it was a clean job
except of course this bit of fur"

most peculiar
no signs of a struggle
the pool water is rippled
this one's a bit of a juggle

this must've been recent
yet not a footprint around
who could've done this
without even touching the ground?

okay let's think
put the pieces together
the birdfeeder's abandoned
in such beautiful weather

this silence is eerie
shh, everyone freeze
there's a faint overhead clicking
high up in the trees

i can't see a thing
the Sun is too bright
partner stay focused
yes, her t-shirt is tight

wait a second, that's it
well, maybe just a guess
if i'm right keep it quiet
this cannot hit the press

that paint job is fresh
the one there on the pink
i don't think a human
would use berries for ink

i've seen this before
though i've made nothing of it
but suddenly in this moment
it just all seems to fit

a bump from an acorn
on the head of each victim
this time its cap unretrieved
because our killer can't swim

see there near the filter
that's our exhibit A
now what? i don't know
i think we're done for today

snap some shots of her shirt
and its dark red motif
i'm not searching any branches
for a confession on a leaf

i'll write the report
unsolved with no referrals
after all who do you call to bring down
a rough gang of squirrels?

a little horse

7/6/06 10:19am
inspired by "Burnt Offering" 2006 Oil on panel by Amanda Besl

everything seems so still
has the world stopped spinning?
the breeze is gone, the flames have ceased
except the ball of fire from the east

i am the last to find this place
no children here, no glowing face
no reason to open an empty case
what happened here has been erased

the years for me move on and on
the dancing orange sheds my skin
all these endings laying on the ashen floor
the smell of which stains every pore

the tears will ask but i won't force
i'm feeling numb and drained and spent
calmer winds and a change of course
won't free me from having to pay rent
the final day of a long divorce
pushes me further from getting a grip, making a dent
and now the ending of a wooden horse
makes me realize i'm not who i meant

short film

8/19/06 12:02am
partly inspired by "Babydoll" 2006 Oil on panel by Amanda Besl

where have you gone?
i got to see you only once
and i'm trying so hard to hold on
to that moment, that image of you
but the Sun pierces my eyelids
and all is awash
from brightness to black
with glowing speckles and sparkles
and soon i'll have to open my blues
and see that you're nowhere around
at once my face was warm in the Sun
with you on my mind
but now it faces the ground
my heart's sweetness now rind
so quick, so cruel
such an unfortunate fool
these lips so want to be kissed
such a short time to be missed
but i won't forget
with my fingers tied tight
several times over
until the end of the spool

untitled
8/20/06 9:26am

What would my days be if you were still here?
Why must we let go more than we get to hold on?

faster

9/22/06 1:09am

you still hold me in my dreams
barely together at the seams
in this unending flow of streams
these words of you fill countless reams

each time you are so real
your skin is warm to feel
i can't defend, you break the seal
your haunting beautiful appeal

i try to calm this new attack
my eyes are closed, i'm in the sack
my battered heart begins to crack
there's no escape, you pull me back

yet i would willingly give in
and let you push me down to pin
take this man and get the win
and hear a beat inside the tin

will this life bring me to you?
the roads are tough on every shoe
distances diminish every clue
soon clouding up my skies of blue

i would love you till we're dust
but i'm not your passion or your lust
i'm discontinued, alone to rust
scattered to nothing by the slightest gust

all i want is for you to know
how it is within your glow
finding me behind the show
to start again but not on slow

these memories test my every nerve
in a daze my tires swerve
hope can't reach your every curve
my love remains deep in reserve

stuck

10/15/06 12:24am
inspired by "Saturday Morning" 2006 Oil on panel by Amanda Besl

oh my it's hot, it's oh so hot
why am i sitting here in this heat?
the car is off, the windows down
this dripping gown melting in this seat

i've already lost my shirt and slacks
i don't care if passers-by's eyes grow wide
i'm dying man, the air is heavy
please break the levy and bring the tide

too tired to think, to feel, to breathe
my brain is frying with a constant hum
all this while he's within the cool
awfully long you fool to get a pack of gum

not much longer before i remove my skin
and sit here just inside my bones
i'd gladly trade this beat-up wreck
heck, just for a couple ice cream cones

if he's not back soon i'll turn to dust
a pair of undies with red dots
and my favorite socks with ruffled trim
it's because of not for him that i've got the hots

oh here he comes with a stupid smile
reminding me why they call him Buck
move over? i can't you big mean jerk
won't work, my back, the seat, i'm glued, they're stuck

nostalgia

10/30/06 10:15pm

I recently drove into New York City to see a show at Carnegie Hall. It was a bit of a drive from Orange County. Took me about an hour and a half with traffic. Not too bad. It's always a good feeling driving over the GW anticipating the night that lies ahead in the city that never sleeps. From the bridge I got on the Henry Hudson and during the ride I would occasionally glance over at the water, the lights in the buildings across the Hudson, the familiar billboards, signs, advertisements, new construction, and the old buildings that never seem to change. There's something comforting in that last one. A constant. Something still there. Something other than a pothole.

I turned on the radio in the car. 880 AM to be exact. I listened to the news, the traffic, the weather. Every day, every hour, every moment the voices on AM tell something different. Always an update in this ever evolving city. Always moving. Always pulsing. There's static. Not much though. It clears up as traffic moves forward.

This drive found me with a grin. So many memories of driving into the city, me as the passenger and younger. My father at the wheel. So many destinations. The Hayden Planetarium. The Beacon Theatre. The Jacob Javitz Center. A Jazz concert outside J&R Music World. Katz's Deli on East Houston Street. The Jazz Standard. The Time Cafe. The Iridium. The MOMA. The Met. HMV. The Blue Note. Lincoln Center. So many shows. So many events. So many people. So much movement. So many lights. So many taxis. A metallic forest. A mecca. Always bright-eyed. Always looking for a spot. "It's only a 14 block walk, but we found a great spot."

Carnegie Hall was fantastic. It was an amazing show! But it all felt nostalgic. Something was missing. Someone was missing. Do we become more of an adult when we travel in the path of our fathers? When we realize that our fathers are part of us in ways that take time to reveal themselves? The city is a place of richness of history and diversity. For me, the magic of the city is so many things, but mainly the memories I have of being there with my father. And sometimes, even more than the city itself, it was the ride in the car to get there. Just me, my father, and our time together on our way to the city that never sleeps.

drawing a heart

11/5/06 11:47pm
inspired by the picture i took for the cover of this book

it's both warm and true
when the heart finds its place
with your feet on the ground
and that look on your face

if you listen and wait
you may just hear a beat
though across more than a state
our words still journey to meet

tears were real as am i
still missing you to the core
i guess we don't all find our way
the current keeps us from the shore

so i sit and i trace
a very familiar shape
in several minutes of grace
pieces come together with tape

a red magic marker
can only fill it with ink
unlike the feeling of you
that can erupt in a blink

your name brings a smile
your voice tingles the spine
you're sweet beyond measure
and these words of mine

what is beautiful?

2/13/07

What is beautiful?

It's so easy to see how beautiful you are on the surface, but I wonder how many people have felt what's really in your heart? Yet somehow, I have. It's something I will never forget. It happened not too long ago when you and I were speaking on the phone; two distant voices connected by a fragile thread. I can still remember the words as I spoke them, "I love you." It took so much to say them, but then again, they just seemed to flow from me as if you were near. And as I said those three words I heard something that was more beautiful than anything I could have ever imagined. I heard your heart. I heard it through your tears. I heard it from deep within you. Within your warmth. Within your glow. It was something so genuine, so beautiful.

All these years I've missed being a part of your life. But who am I? A distant voice? A memory? Will I ever get to find you again? I hope that one day, if only once, I can feel your arms around me so that you can hear my heart.

I miss you.

again
5/27/07 11:18am

i haven't seen you in how long now?
how long has it been?
you left as quickly as the clouds did
on that warm, windy day
my wondrous warrior with freckled skin

yet i still think of you
and how i never got the chance
to feel the depths of your heart
as i hold on tight
and my breathing finds its feet to dance

you will never be forgotten
the you behind that beautiful face
so foolish was i
to never once have kissed that skin
but you tangled my laces and ended the chase

only one of you in this lonely orb
reaffirming that life is bittersweet
is it better to have known you than not at all?
yes a million times in this spinning circle
with ends again to meet?

misstep

6/2/07 11:35pm

why must i dream so much?
well, because she can't possibly be real
so i close my eyes and find my crutch
but the alarm clock blares and breaks the seal

my eyes open to meet a blazing sun
blinding me with its new old hello
my days are bleeding into this stale so-called fun
outside my front door the ruthless get-up-and-go

answers tend to hide right in plain sight
but seemingly only for those who know these streets
my questions find me alone, consumed by the night
the concert of my heart plays to empty seats

i just can't find my rhythm, outside of myself
guess i'm just an outsider, the familiar a blur
too many useless how-to's on too many a shelf
the haunted truth of each pinpointed slip-up and slur

so i'll dream until my days are old
and i no longer recall the hurt, the pain
except for fleeting moments when the fog loses its hold
and i see her face again in my world, my tears, the rain

water and earth

6/4/07 12:17am (*6/8/07 12:49am)
inspired by "Splash" 2007 Oil on panel by Amanda Besl

yuck, splat, how about that?
an old muddy road and now a mud covered hat

slosh, squish, my turn for a wish
i want to flop, jump, and twitch like a boot wearin' fish

ick, no guess, this is clearly a mess
i'll need a torch to remove all the dirt from this dress

*spray, splotch, turn your head, don't watch
this is too much fun not to raise it a notch

with a slick dirt sheen, now i'll never be clean
one foot in the brown, the other landing on green

tumble and whirl, not a couch-farin' girl
get your hands in the land and out comes a pearl

what a day, you and i, me and you and the sky
a push and a laugh, a run and a chase, a girl and a guy

miracles

6/23/07 3:22pm

miracles are paid in full when the stars go out
when the Sun goes cold
and by then the memory of what it's all about
will have wrinkled and yellowed and lost its hold

first
6/27/07 12:14am

the first kiss
the first taste
a flood of warmth
above the waist

her eyes deep
a tight embrace
her skin soft
a smiling face

so bittersweet
beneath the lace
slow the speed
extend the race

my first kiss
my first taste
of eager lips
so move the furniture with haste
my heart needs the space

submerged

7/8/07 1:20am

your skin has me trapped
i'm completely surrounded
a moment ago i was free
now battlestation alerts have been sounded

i dive deep within
all the signals are flashing
the force jostles the current
the waves meet the shore with a crashing

my breath no longer my own
as i head towards the source
the sonar dances in blips
with my heart pounding in morse

weapons are loaded and hot
with hopes that they are precise
although in this heated battle
the sweat involved will entice

my white flag of surrender
was left home on the dryer
soon i'll be spent and defeated
while a flood i'll perspire

i lay back to recover
from the rush and the ending
the time for revenge is at hand
my desire building and pending

my purple heart still is beating
i wear it on my chest
that you reached out and shined it
i never would have guessed

spiderweb
7/26/07 8:49pm

the air is damp from the passing storm
the lamp lights glisten in the remnants of rain
that shutter as i pass down the concrete path
washed clean of young weeds, leaving a hint of green stain

making my way up the stairs of old weathered wood
i stop at the top only feet from the door
my keys jingle in my hand though far from December
as i stare at this newly made arachnid decor

drops of rain are suspended, barely hanging on
to this silken weaving of intricate design
what an amazing exhibit, a sight to be seen
yet strangely here i am, the only one waiting in line

but i really don't mind that there isn't a crowd
it's just me and an eight legged artist of sorts
the mosquitos however aren't here for the show
they're quite hungry, i can tell because i'm wearing shorts

so i duck and i twist, open close i'm inside
i'm tired from the day and in need of my bed
the noise and the rush turns to silence and calm
there's comfort in easing the neural web in my head

morning arrives, bright and early, as it usually does
the normal routine on my mind as i leave for work
i open the door and meet the spiderweb with my face
and i swear that i hear from somewhere overhead
the tiniest voice say, "You jerk!"

blank page

the contents of an unlikely story

8/28/07 1:14am (*8/28/07 12:21am)
this ending written on the date of her beginning

Each ember dances from this dying fire; a burning void, golden and glowing; but I stare too long and the flames dance in threes; a sort of triple vision of flowing light. The sight has me pondering, "Will my life end in an endless heat or will my final days ahead be consumed by the cold?" The days are rushing by faster than I can speak my mind. Increasing my words per minute will only serve to make conversations impossible to understand. The friction of which won't be enough to bring heat to this chill. I'm here alone, stranded, as the others chose to keep driving on to find some secluded and perhaps abandoned drive-in where old faded posters hype an esoteric flick from some distant past. Oh how such places were once lit up with life and energy; now only dark and still.

As the fire puffs out its remaining light, the flies glow and buzz through the nightscape until they vanish into the surrounding darkness. This place is always the same through the seasons, through the ages. It's so quiet here now. I refocus my thoughts to the babble of my days, my hours, minutes. The concert of nothing. Well, except for maybe a ringing in my ears. There's no one to talk to. Besides, what's the point of silent letters when no one is around to hear the words they form? Am I someone important? Are we what we are when we close our eyes and wait until dawn to see again? I'm feeling a bit existential. Maybe I'm just hungry. So many questions. I'm tired.

The new day finds me walking along some train tracks, feeling the ground rumble as each iron beast passes. Different trains run through with so many eyes watching through glass the land go by in a blur. Too fast to notice a fallen bird or other scenes from the road I find myself standing on, as the train disappears. Ten cars total, swallowed by the land. I've never been in this town before. I must've been walking for hours. However, things here aren't that different from any other town. Even the garbage bag under a yield sign doesn't strike me as odd. I don't know exactly what's in it? There's a slight chance that if I looked I'd find my other sock.

Now, before i forget, I need to find a bookstore and pick up a copy of "Mr. Me And Miss You;" a quick read with lots of pictures. As I walk I see some red, exotic, European sports car parked in front of a thrift shop. It's a nice car with what used to be a moth now splattered on the windshield. Imagine fluttering around until zap, flash, death. Do you even know what that would be like? Does anyone? What if that happened to me? Improbable? Yes. Well, at least in this universe. What a strange thought. Maybe not as strange as me here talking to myself. The license plate says KRIS on it. We put our names on so many things. Most of them seem to be shiny.

I stop for a minute as my mind switches over to thinking of you. I'm here on this strange street, in the open air, feeling wondrous. Now I need a place to sit. I think that doing so would please my feet, if only for a bit. But I don't want to sit here. I want to sit on an old, wooden bench on a hill overlooking fields where the pollen rides the breeze. There I can close my eyes and listen as my mind remembers the letter I sent her. I never did get her reply. I gasp. Everything goes black.

I open my eyes to find that I'm lying on the sidewalk. It's dark. Somehow I like this feeling of finding something new every time I open my eyes on this journey. For now I'll just breathe in the night air and let it cool my lungs. How did I get here? I look skyward to find it starless. Not even any lights from an airplane in flight. Who turned off the sky? The last time this happened it was just a dream, but am I dreaming now? I can't grasp the scope of this moment. Where am I? Where is this town? Where is it on a map? Where is it on a map of time and space? My arms are shaking. It's cold outside, but I'm burning up. Why bother fighting this sudden warmth in my veins? I put my hand on my forehead. This fever could be a trap. Soon I could be drowning in sweat. Maybe I should take some kind of action. Something daring? I should call my home number and see if I'm there sleeping, but what would I say to myself after the beep? I'm starting to worry and still I do nothing. I just stand with poor posture. I notice a crumpled piece of paper on the ground. I pick it up. It looks like an old telegram. It says LAURA. Someone real? A ghost? Then it just says love, stop. I try to read the rest, but it's smudged.

I think I'll find a room for the night, or at least what's left of this bizarre evening. I find an inn. It seems inviting with a candle lit walkway leading towards a red brick entrance with a brown, weathered door. I take the only remaining quarters and say a quiet goodnight. Anybody listening is keeping it to themselves. Untitled are the echoes that find their way around each and every corner of this place. To stay here too long would be to wither and crumble and find oneself a part of the wind and shore that can be seen from the deck on the other side of the building.

Words can carry meaning and desire, but not the metal and feathers found in the kitchen as I make my way towards the smell of food. It's morning. Winter is here. I haven't left yet. I've lost track of the calendar. I know that something in this place will click with my brain so I can save the connection I once had to what's real. I look down at my plate and its binary arrangement of breakfast. Two eggs. Two strips of bacon and sausage. Two pieces of toast. I open the morning paper to find that some local superhero, Super Paint Girl, was spotted saving the world, or at least this corner of it. Another article talks about an upcoming book about this resident do-gooder, as yet untitled. There's a story about why bugs will outlive us all. It's a strange story, yet I don't see why a theory is needed to prove the obvious? Take a seat rocket scientists. I think you need a snapshot of common sense and then boom, you'll see it too. You don't need a fancy machine to see what's so clear. Nature may be untame, but that doesn't mean there's no more hope in trying to find truth.

An article near the bottom of the page has a short title. It just says PRECIP. Probably something about the weather. Even a newspaper has nothing better to talk about. Just a bunch of words and flies in my face. Get away from my bacon! Fine. Here you go. Now leave me alone. They will outlive us all if we keep giving them our bacon. I guess I'm no good at being selfish. Too late. I ate it all. From A to B. From plate to mouth. A full stomach makes my eyes grow heavy. I find a bench near the window and lay down.

After a while I feel a shaking, a stirring. I wake to find the countryside speeding by. It's daytime, but the air is thick with mist. I'm in a compartment on a padded bench. When did time put me here? Outside everything looks dull and worn from this train ride through the gray of this new day. I reduce the sight in my mind to a mixture of light and time. What is it really? Just a feeling of motion? Just shapes? Just words?

It's a lonely ride, yet somehow hope exists behind the fog. If I could only find the joy behind the solitude. Darn that dream I had the other night when you came to my room in that perfect dress and I was so taken by everything that was you. My solitude turns to tranquility as if just the thought of you sends a run program command to my heart drive. Searching. Searching for the file. Same old me. If only I remembered to put it back where it belongs. Just because your memory stays with me, doesn't mean that today will be the day that I find a clue as to where I put the shoe box containing that necklace of desire you once wanted. Or is it just that I never gave it to you because you were never real? Why did our final page in the story of us have to end so abruptly? I was left broken.

The spiders left a small web in the corner of the window near where I'm sitting. If I were a ninja ballerina I could flick it away with my toe, but I've got more important things to sort through in my head; such as the questions, "Does Robin sometimes wish he could say goodbye to Batman and start his own crime-fighting business? Would he want nothing else to do with Gotham and go and find his own turf?" I guess he could ride in on a little horse with matching colors. If it ever became a movie it would be quite a short film. They'd probably have to keep it untitled to throw Batman off the scent. Besides, without Robin, Batman would most certainly move faster. And then Robin would end up being stuck without a partner and without an Oscar and be left sitting around with a sense of nostalgia.

Strange thoughts on this train ride. I find myself drawing a heart on the window after a long warm breath creates my canvas. What is beautiful here? Again I wonder about the landscape's lack of color on this gloomy day. Where am I headed? I can't quite trace the path that got me here. Was there a misstep in my direction? The only constant has been that of water and earth. Has each new moment been that of miracles or of time just pulling me along? First I need to breathe. A deep breath. So here I am, submerged in the air within this train car, speeding off to somewhere with me in its belly.

The spiderweb seems to just move and flow with the world, with the movement of all this metal and steel. I think I'll play along. Let's see where I end up. I need to find life. I need it to find me. See, *I've been dying since the day I broke your heart. All those years ago in that quiet room, on that dark street, near the glittering surface of that lake that looked like an ocean…

squint

10/3/07 1:26am

hope has failed
hope that i would get to be in your arms again
hope that i could experience more with you
hope that you'd open your heart to me
hope that i could make you feel as beautiful as you are
hope that you could feel wanted, held, loved with me
hope that we wouldn't be alone anymore
hope that my affection for you would be returned
so much hope
yet i'm left cold, sad
and you seem so far away
there's so much warmth with you
happiness
it could be so simple
but the three most wonderful words i gave to you
are without an echo
my arms are without yours
my lips are without yours
my body is without yours
my love is without yours
hope has failed

yet you are loved
and always will be

cleaning heart

10/6/07 11:41am

she's far away
a long drive, almost an hour
through two counties, or three
and over a bridge
such a long car ride alone with my thoughts of her
it's been a long time since i last saw her
that night we spent together
keeps repeating in my brain
sending waves of remembering her skin, her touch
through my body
a chill
i grip the wheel and try to keep the car inside the lines
why isn't love simple?
i guess if it was then her arms would be on my shoulders
finding us in a kiss
but her heart is protected by armor
though there'll be no duel today
she's home, cleaning her house
removing the memory of us from her front door?
from her couch?
from the stairs leading up?
from the hallway?
from her bed?
from her body?
from her life?
she's far away
and my love for her is reduced to this ink,
these words
which may never find her eyes

what would it be like?

10/9/07 6:01am

what would it be like
to get into my car after a night at work
and drive to exit four?

what would it be like
to find an open gate
a right, a left, and then an open door?

what would it be like
to let go of the day
and all its empty cares?

what would it be like
to shut the lights, ease the mind
and make my way upstairs?

what would it be like
to slide into bed
slowly passing your feet, your hips?

what would it be like
when you start to smile
as i gently kiss your lips?

what would it be like
to slide under the covers
as our arms all wrap around?

what would it be like
to sigh in the comfort
of this feeling that's been found?

what would it be like
to know that at any moment
my hand can find your skin?

what would it be like
to have each day's ending
leave off where we begin?

what would it be like
to not be bothered
with the morning stopping by?

what would it be like
to feel you close and touch your hand
as the Sun swims through the sky?

what would it be like
to feel you pull me to you
in such a warm embrace?

what would it be like
to know that only a day
lies between returning to this place?

what would it be like
to have pieces fit
instead of life pulling them apart?

what would it be like
to know that every minute that passes by
i'm alive within your heart?

check please

12/10/07 2:59am

my footprints are covered
in the drifting of snow
and the cold bitterness
of your heart letting go

alone, now it's winter
now your warmth doesn't show
to know such highs in your arms
stripped down to a low

i love you, i love you
every inch, head to toe
but i'm not the one that you love
here, far away from your glow

you've left me all broken
are these tears soon to slow?
just one you, bittersweet
and a table for one by the window
with my now cold cup of joe

feverish fields

7/5/08 9:38pm
written with a fever of 102°

my thoughts feel uneven
when the fever grows high
am i awake in a nightmare
or asleep in a daydream
walking through fields of uncertainty
unsure if it's night or now day
or just a headache from the overwhelming scent
of these flowers blooming crooked on their brain stems
is that a clearing up ahead or just the edge of my bed
i don't know, i don't know
i'm either covered in sweat or just feeling the stain
of the evidence of rain washing me sane
and soaking this plain as my numbers go up
it sure is hot here yet there is a breeze
somewhere off to the side
oscillating and whirring it teases my face
where in the world am i
are my insides in hell
while my skin takes a stroll
well if it happens to notice a market
please bring a cool drink to my soul
a day or a week
this is outside of time
all the shivering and shaking under these sweat-filled covers
with my eyes wide open under the most beautiful sky
my vision won't tell me what i'm really seeing
and my camera phone is miles away on the nightstand
i can't figure this out
this program won't let me save
my printer gives me an error
there's no wi-fi in my grave
i'll just have to hang on
i'll just have to be brave
crap, is that my alarm clock or an explosion
is it monday already
everything is so blurry
i can barely make out a face looking back at me
i'm either being threatened by captors
or i'm now trying to shave

applesauce

7/5/08 10:35pm

what will i learn in my dreams tonight
will my eyelids be shut while their insides seem bright
and as my temperature rises will the covers feel tight
do secrets unfold if bedbugs take a bite

what will i find in the heat flow of my mind
will the burning ash of memory glow evil or kind
and will i be left with myself or seared down to the rind
my defenses are trapped, this twist-tie won't unwind

what will i be when this runs its full course
will the screaming subside or ride off on a horse
will the brain and the body stay linked or divorce
and is there a long enough probe for the wacks to find the source

so what will be in the end or am i just applesauce
laying here roasting while my body grows moss
somehow the world keeps on spinning with me in the bin labeled loss
a nice shiny sticker, a fresh coat of gloss

hollow

3/1/09 2:47am

my shell
empty now
hollow
a heart
borrowed
keys
taken
car
missing
you
come back
please
make me whole again

i was happy

3/28/09 11:38pm

i was happy earlier today
i was happy because the weather was warm
and i was in love

i was happy because my favorite ice-cream
was on sale at the supermarket
and i was in love

i was happy because there was no work to be done
it was Saturday
and i was in love

i was happy because my girlfriend
just called me on the phone
and we were in love

i was happy until she told me
that we were through
we used to be in love

then she hung up
and she was gone

i was happy earlier today

not anymore.

aquamarine

4/17/09 7:40pm, (*6/17/09 2:54pm)

aquamarine, how did i find you?

*i wasn't even looking
for a way through the fog
with my life in the dirt
minutes turning to hours
each night with me on the couch
is this all that i have?
the blaring tv
with nothing good on at three
the hours just blur into time's lonely sea

and then one day you appear
my heart remembers you here
and what only seems to happen in stories
has happened to me

days become weeks
finally safe with spaces filled in
and a heart full of red
as your arms pull me close
we can't see the couch from my bed
my aquamarine
i'll love you for as long as the sky is blue

weeks become months
but before i get the chance
to combine you with a ring
a last kiss much too short
and the fog finds me in spring

where'd we go wrong my aquamarine?

how did i lose you?

no love

6/14/09 5:38pm

even when her love feels real
there is no love

even when in her arms you heal
there is no love

even when sweet words find her tears
there is no love

even when days feel like years
there is no love

even when you've touched her heart
there is no love

even when you've kissed every part
there is no love

even when her smile is just for you
there is no love

and now she's left my days a darker hue
because she told me, "sorry, there is no love."

www.ingramcontent.com/pod-product-compliance
Lightning Source LLC
Chambersburg PA
CBHW051803040426
42446CB00007B/490